DANG DISTRACTIONS

15 Distractions Aimed to Deter and Discourage... And What to Do About Them

Chrystal Epps-Bean

⚓
Anchored
Redemption
Publishing
Anchored Redemption, LLC
2021 ©

Dang Distractions
15 Distractions Aimed to Deter and Discourage...
And What to Do About Them

Anchored Redemption, LLC © 2021

First Printing: 2021
Printed in the United States of America
ISBN 978-1-7347310-8-8
Anchored Redemption, LLC
PO Box 1031
Cordova, TN 38088

www.anchoredredemption.com

Ordering Information: Special discounts are available on quantity purchases. For details, contact the publisher at the above listed address.

Introduction

Do you ever feel stagnated in life, or feel like you're not going anywhere? Are you achieving your dreams, or do you feel as though your goals are stuck at the starting line, despite you moving and working hard? Have you ever started something but didn't finish—or initiated but never followed through? It could be the distractions of life that are holding you back and keeping you from getting to the finish line. To gain traction and move forward effectively, you must recognize distractions for what they are and rid yourself of them as much as possible. This book will help you to *recognize the enemies of focus* so that you can *regain* a firm footing to *reach* the finish line of your goals and dreams.

"A ferocious concentration and a fanatical execution are what you need to finish strong." – Gary Ryan Blair

Contents

Chapter 1

Distractions Defined

D etours, deviations, diversions, disturbances, disappointments, divisions, and disruptions all encapsulate one big dose of distraction(s). Many people prescribe to distractions and welcome these inhibiting disruptors because of the need to keep up, fit in, please people, and placate personal desires. Oftentimes, to one's liking, distractions taste pleasant—flavoring life with busyness yet unproductiveness, and a pinch of deceit, all the while chocking up your destiny and aiming to deplete your power. Consequently, distracted-prone individuals become a bullseye for bondage, and get knocked down by the sharp darts of distraction every time.

Distractions often come with a form of deceit... instead of distractions being an action, they're actually an inaction that stagnates your purpose and stifles your dreams.

Activity does not always equal productivity. Busyness does not always equate to fruitfulness.

Let's start off by defining a distraction. A distraction is anything that prevents someone from giving full and total attention to something more important. The eclectic nature of distractions is what makes them so destructive. For instance, there are internal distractions such as anger, depression, doubt, worry, fear, jealousy, bitterness and insecurities, and there are external distractions such as financial issues, relationship issues, people and their unrelenting requests and agendas, TV, social media, peer pressure, tensions, wars, natural disasters, sickness, disease, and the list goes on. This all sounds like a clear description of life, right? For many, distractions have become idols, inhibitions, and intrusions—a way of life that keeps many stressed and stymied.

The distractions of life, replete with twists, turns and short-lived smooth sailing, operate under the guise of desires, discouragement and pseudo demands. Distractions are the enemy of purpose, the diversions of **destiny**, that seek to knock us off course. Everyone was created with a purpose and for a purpose. But if you are always distracted, you will never know what your purpose is or will struggle to live it out.

"Protect your purpose by prioritizing and managing your priorities. You must develop priorities as they protect you from other people managing your life. Without priorities, you will end up living other people's priorities." – Dr. Myles Munroe

Managing distractions is not about being flexible but about being firm about how you spend your time.

We all know how busy life can get. You start taking steps, then life gets hectic; you start again running, then adversity hits; you begin to gain a little momentum, and boom... disaster strikes! You finally get up again and start moving, only to get distracted by the loss, lusts, and longings of life...working tirelessly to earn, deal with problems, fit in, and impress—styling, smiling, and profiling. When does it end? It ends when you take a stand and make a conscious decision to get things done, no matter what—or when you choose to make "it" happen and not allow everything to happen in the midst of making it happen, or "it" won't happen.

When you really think about it, our world is built upon laws, statutes, policies, procedures, rules, protocols, penalties, punishment, and discipline—which are all aimed to maintain order and mitigate distractions and disruptions. Every organization, workplace and entity have rules, guidelines, and standards in place for this very reason. By the same token, standards and boundaries must be established in your life (your world), to maintain proper order with minimal distractions.

Dis-traction

'Dis' means to divide or separate from, creating a dichotomy from the main cause or purpose. For instance, when you dis-respect, you lose respect; when you dis-connect, you lose connection, and when you yield to dis-tractions, you lose traction and throttle down the momentum to your purpose and destiny—dis-abling or losing your ability to achieve your maximum potential. You must remain cognizant and wise about how you deal with distractions and recognize them for what they are. If you don't, your spirit will become increasingly dis-couraged and dis-quieted to the extent that you'll lose courage, calm and peace. A distracted mind is a divided mind.

Let's establish what distractions are, and what they are not. Distractions are the opposite of duties, hence; if something is a duty, it is not a distraction, and if something is a distraction, it is not a duty. Below are some examples of duties:

- It is your duty to love God, yourself, and others.
- It is your duty to take care of your family and home—to serve your husband/wife and children, contribute to your family's inheritance and build a meaningful legacy.
- It is your duty to take care of yourself, improve yourself, and invest in your future.
- It is your duty to earn a living with dignity and excellence.
- It is your duty to live out your purpose and achieve your goals and dreams.

- It is your duty to grow, learn, and acquire wisdom and knowledge.
- It is your duty to act responsibly—to do what is right and do it right.
- It is your duty to become a productive citizen of society by obeying the law, serving, and contributing to a momentous cause(s).
- It is your duty to manage all of these—be a good steward of your time, set limits and boundaries, establish standards, and prioritize.

Fulfilling your duties is a bullseye on the target.

A "devotion to duty" will get you to your goal. Therefore, be obligated to duties, and not subservient to distractions.

Duties are rooted in purpose, while distractions are often designed to deter you from purpose.

Distractions are deterrents that prevent you from hitting life's targets centered on success. Success is not about how much money you have, who you know, or your title, position, or possessions. Success is achieving your purpose, goals, and destiny undeterred despite the deterrents. A deterrent is anything that is not a duty—hence, a distraction.

Therefore:

- It is not a duty to engulf yourself in countless hours of television, social media, and frivolous living. DISTRACTION
- It is not a duty to say 'Yes' to every request. DISTRACTION [NO is okay to say]
- It is not a duty to spend time hating, envying, deceiving, or trying to impress and please people. DISTRACTION
- It is not a duty to operate in greed and excessive self-indulgence. DISTRACTION
- It is not a duty to fit in or seek to be liked. DISTRACTION
- It is not a duty to live life haphazardly and behave inattentively. DISTRACTION

Distractions are ubiquitous—they are everywhere, and manifest in the form of people, events, situations, selfish desires, insecurities, feelings/emotions, indecisions, thoughts, wrong perceptions, and imaginations.

Oftentimes, you'll get pulled in many directions when everyone and everything places their demands on you; it feels good to be needed, but for the sake of sanity, sometimes you must pull back and release yourself.

Distractions deter focus...
Focus fosters your future.

True success is having goals and hitting your targets (no matter how big or small they arc) with intentionality and intensity of focus.

"Success is a moving target... it's different for everybody and each person has to learn to define their own. Otherwise, they are always trying to fulfill somebody else's plan." – Mary Crowley

The primary reasons for distractions are to discourage you and to get you to *forget* what really matters—to cause you to lose focus and get you off track. Distractions are a colossal waste of your time, leading you closer to your expiration date without significant achievement, accomplishment, or acquisition.

The Golden Rule when it comes to distractions is:

Duty first, self second.

In other words, the only time you should really entertain a time-consuming distraction is when you have fulfilled your duties. Duties do not belong in your peripheral vision; they belong at the center of your focus.

Millionaires and billionaires are not born;
they are simply the manifestation of the distractions they
denied, and the time and resources
they effectively managed.

Do whatever you have to do to rid yourself of distractions. When you are faced with a distraction:

- Call it out for what it is*—a 'Dang Distraction'
- Catch the outliers
- Cancel disruptions
- Cease your inner chatterbox
- Censor negative thoughts and discussions
- Cherish your time
- Choose your duty
- Close the door on ambient noise and drama
- Combat internal conflict
- Command your day
- Commit to greater efforts
- Consciously decide on productivity, positivity, and progress
- Control your destiny
- Counteract inertia
- Cultivate positive change
- Cut it off or cut her/him off

Your decisions determine your destiny.

*Whenever I find myself diverting from a task to look at, listen to or do something else that doesn't align with my task or duty, I say to myself (or out loud when no one is around) ... "Distraction!". This is my way of calling it out for what it is. I then immediately get back on track and finish completing the task. *Self-discipline is the best discipline.*

The antitheses of distractions are *discipline, diligence,* and *discernment.* You must be consciously aware and compunctious about how you spend your time. *When you live with purpose, you become a gatekeeper of your time and realize that it is valuable and essential to your destiny.* If you do not manage your time, your time will manage you. Planning and prioritizing are essential to demolishing distractions, exercising your duties, and achieving your destiny.

Potential distractions are often embedded in your decisions. You activate distractions when you <u>choose</u> to yield to them; you deactivate distractions when you <u>choose</u> to turn away.

We've all heard the catchphrase "time is money"; however, sometimes it is not about the money but about making everything balance. Anyone in the finance world knows the importance of making things balance, particularly numbers and a balanced budget. If the total is off—under or over, even if it is only 10 cents, it throws everything off. It's not necessarily about the 10 cents (it won't make or break the budget) but about making everything jibe.

In the same manner, it is not necessarily about the hour you wasted because you allowed yourself to be distracted, but about making sure your duties are balanced. If one hour prevents you from fulfilling a duty for the day, it throws your level of productivity off balance and may push you back a day, a week, or longer—in proportion to the length and level of the distraction(s). Be not deceived; distractions can generate a definite deficit (significant shortfall) that is both cumulative and costly. Over time, the impact could become evident in failed relationships, unfinished projects, missed deadlines, unused potential, impeded improvement, postponed purpose, and deterred destiny. Audit and balance your time—your greatest asset.

Distractions are no balancing act; this would mean all things equal—or duties on the same level as distractions. Put distractions in their proper place by eliminating or permitting them at the appropriate time... putting the most important things first.

You must balance and prioritize duties; you do not balance distractions. You work them in, and only allow distractions at a time that is amenable to your schedule.

Moreover, unbalanced living stems from unbalanced actions. Many people fire before they ready themselves and aim. Others go, before they get *ready* and *set* their mind to achieve. If one does not aim, and instead approaches the target area willy-nilly, one cannot expect to hit the center— the bullseye on the target. As a result, there will be a lot of rework, corrective action, restructuring, wasted time and energy, wasted dollars, and sadly sometimes, a wasted life.

The proper order and formulation as we all know it is: *Ready, aim, fire; Get ready, get set, go.*

Distractions divide and transpose the right course of action because they deter or limit focus, catalyze poor planning, and encourage a half-hearted approach.

You won't hit a target that you're not aiming for or when you approach the target off-kilter.

Deadweight Distractions

Economists refer to the term deadweight loss as the inefficient allocation of resources where both parties lose—the suppliers and the demanders. With deadweight distractions, nobody wins, not the person who allows themselves to be distracted (supplier) and not the person or thing that demands or draws the supplier's attention. For example, a deadweight loss could involve a person who is distracted by binge-watching TV on their favorite streaming service platform for 8 hours a day. No one wins. The distracted person has lost valuable time that they could have used to do something more productive; and the streaming service provider gained nothing by the binge watching—they still got paid their monthly subscription fee, regardless if the person binge watched or not... deadweight loss.

In another instance, consider a family friend who called you while you were spending quality time with your family (fulfilling a duty). She needs help moving furniture and asked that you come over within the next hour before she leaves for work. As a friend, you could consider it your duty to help a friend in need, or you could view this as a distraction because this is not an urgent or life-altering matter. Regardless, helping your friend to move furniture would not be a deadweight distraction entirely because your friend received your help, and you were able to go back home to spend quality time with your family. But say for instance, your friend called and changed her mind as you were in route. This, however, could be a deadweight loss because nobody won or gained anything.

An investment of time is not always a total loss, although time is lost in the sense that you can never get it back. The outcome and your perspective of time expended relative to the circumstances determines the state of your return on investment (ROI).

In the latter example, helping your friend or attempting to help her could be viewed positively to the extent that it was an investment of time in the friendship. Or, as forementioned, it could be viewed negatively as a deadweight loss depending on the nature of the friendship and circumstances.

Friendships can be a "limited" duty and a good investment when both sides consistently make deposits into the relationship. Otherwise, it could just be a deadweight loss or a deadweight distraction.

"The leech has two suckers that cry out, "More, more!" [1]

Deadweight is much heavier than the original weight of its subject. Supporting a friendship or relationship is hard enough, but when someone selfishly and manipulatively adds excess baggage, requests, and demands without deposits, he/she could become a deadweight loss—draining your power and depleting your energy and resources. In this instance, nobody wins when it is at the full expense of another person.

"A stone is heavy and sand is weighty, but resentment caused by a fool is even heavier." [2]

Sacrificing oneself, however, for the greater good even when it seems as if you are losing is a winning way—a delegated duty, that when executed generates enduring and sometimes eternal deposits.

Curious Curves—Beneficial Diversions

Curiosity can lead to serendipitous discoveries and foster great change when sparked with the right intentions.

In some cases, curiosity can deter you from a focused task. And sometimes, curiosity is good and can yield great gains. For example, one day as I was checking my state-sponsored retirement account, I saw a link for unclaimed property which took me to another official website with the state. The site included a database comprised of thousands of people, totaling millions of unclaimed dollars. I instantly got distracted from my main aim (the task at hand which was to check and analyze my account). However, discovering the possibility of claiming money due to me certainly piqued my curiosity. Although I did not find any unclaimed property under my name, allowing myself to be distracted in the discovery of unclaimed money resulted in me finding nearly $500 for my family in just 30 minutes, as I searched their names one by one. Their unclaimed property (money) included refunds from utility and insurance companies that were listed as the "holder type". In this instance, I took a curve from the intended course, but this absolutely proved to be a beneficial diversion—one distraction that I am happy I yielded myself to. All family members received a check within two weeks of submitting their claim. If you live in the U.S., check to see if your state has a treasury of this information and a process for claiming unclaimed dollars.

The key point here is to *quickly analyze distractions as they come and discern the potential value of the distraction* (if any) to determine possible gains and deadweight losses. Cognizance (being keenly aware) and critical thinking (strategizing) are essential to defeating and leveraging distractions.

Through every experience and encounter, glean from it and learn what you can, not only for the benefit of you, but for the sake of others.

Chapter 2
Ethics and Etiquette

E thics and etiquette surrounding the decision to eliminate distractions involve self-discipline, self-analysis, and self-talk. In addition to the ability to convey to others *firmly*, truthfully, and politely your opposition to their interruptions, interjections, insistencies, and intrusions.

1. Evaluate Opportunity Costs

When considering distractions, it is important for you to weigh opportunity costs. Opportunity cost(s) is the difference between what you could have obtained versus what you actually obtained. For instance, if a single parent considers a second job, but chooses to stay at home with her child instead of taking the job, the opportunity cost (what she could have obtained) was extra income for her family. She, however, gave up extra income to spend more time with her child.

To achieve success, we should evaluate the opportunity cost(s) when deciding whether to give in to a distraction. You must be consciously aware and ask yourself: what am I giving up; what duty am I neglecting if I choose to serve this distraction instead of serving my duty and destiny.

Before building a house, every builder calculates the costs, because what sense would it make to start building when there is not enough money to finish the project. Likewise, before you lay the foundation of distraction, consider what it will cost you.

"The cost of a thing is the amount of what I will call life which is required to be exchanged for it, immediately or in the long run." – Henry David Thoreau

2. Expand Your Territory

If you do not limit distractions, distractions will limit you.

One objective to managing and/or eliminating distractions is to expand your territory and engender unlimited success. Your territory—the space that you claim, your piece of the pie, your place in the world, so to speak, encompasses your influence, impact, contributions, ideas, and creations. Your territory marks the indelible footprint that you imprint in the lives of others and in the world paved with your gifts and talents. When you allow yourself to be distracted profusely, you forfeit or lose a lot of territory and give up a lot of ground. But when you manage distractions effectively, you gain ground; and when you push through adversity and conquer the internal distractions of fear, distress, and discouragement, you expand your world... your territory.

3. Consider the Greater Good

When you limit and eliminate distractions, you sacrifice less important things for more important things. You give up what is insignificant for what is and who is more significant.

Distractions are oftentimes *unilateral*. In other words, they involve appeasing oneself or another person(s) selfishly without considering more important things or other people. But when you give up distractions to focus on what is needful and necessary, you employ a *utilitarian* approach as you contribute to the greater good for yourself, your family, and sphere of influence.

When you aim to get your duties done, to make it happen, everyone around you and outside of you can become the beneficiary. To the contrary, when you fail to perform your duties, or fall short of making things happen, everyone around you and outside of you can become collateral damage.

4. Excel at Everything You Do

One motivation to eliminating distractions is to achieve and accomplish with excellence. Excellence requires concentration (focused energy), and concentration requires conscious effort—which in turn yields optimal soundness of mind and the ability to hear yourself think without the internal and external chatter. This sound thinking then informs your decisions and actions. Concentration keeps your train of thought on track without it being diverted by distractions... swerving and turning corners with no real direction. When you lose your *train* of thought, it is hard to find it and put it back on *track*. A person can't excel beyond their short attention span or their ability to concentrate. A short attention span with the proclivity to be easily distracted obstructs excellence. You determine how long or short your span of attention is by choosing to make your internal will and external environment conducive to focus rather than attention deficits and disruptions.

Without extended effort and focused energy, excellence cannot be achieved. Moving without focused energy is like walking on a treadmill—moving but not going anywhere. No matter how much you increase the speed, and no matter how tired and frazzled you become, you are still not going anywhere. You tire yourself out and burn a lot of time and energy by moving in place. When you are not focused, you tend to make mistakes and a pile of *sloppy* joe—a *sloppy* job that no one wants to consume. However, when you are focused, you make less mistakes, especially when you focus on one task at a time, when possible.

"Whatever you do, do well. For when you go to the grave, there will be no work or planning or knowledge or wisdom."[1]

Our goal as capable, intelligent, and purposeful individuals is to *excel in excellence.* Distractions make it difficult to excel and will prevent you from hitting the excellence target because you lack laser-like focus. Excellence doesn't mean perfection, it just means you put your best effort forward and give it everything you've got—a steady aim, a focused mind, a good attitude, and a willful heart to hit the bullseye target of success. Focused people are not perfect, they just manage their imperfections well and apply their strengths and shortcomings to meaningful work without the distractions—this is what it means to truly excel in life.

"... My measure of success is following the game plan designed for that game to the very best of my ability."
— Walter Payton

Furthermore, focused energy cultivates rest because it allows you to get things done more effectively and efficiently versus unfocused energy makes you tired because you are going through the motions with no goal— responding to every request, thinking about everything, being involved in everything with no clear aim, no clear purpose or definite direction. In other words, you are moving but not growing, performing but not transforming—a vision without viability, validity, or clarity of focus; and reacting without rational thought.

Point to Ponder: What is the point of your focus; what are you really aiming for?

It is worth mentioning that some psychologists and self-help books believe that conscious effort inhibits the innate "success mechanism" which operates through the power of the subconscious mind. This may be true; however, conscious effort must still be employed at some point to effectively allow the subconscious to work. For example, set a goal (conscious effort) and allow your internal success mechanism (subconscious) to work for you by guiding you through the actions to achieve the goal.

Just because you move into a brand-new (newly built) house, doesn't mean you won't have rats.

Note that even when you adopt a new way of thinking in terms of valuing your time and choosing to spend it wisely, your environment can still limit you and become a pesky problem. The critters of distraction are not so easy to get rid of, especially when you operate on their territory. If you don't keep your environment clean—time-sensitive, organized and sanitized with purpose, it could become woody and whimsical with clutter and inconsistency. You must be diligent about maintaining proper order. I am not saying you should restrict yourself 100% from distractions but leave an extremely small margin of error for interruptions and disruptions. Of course, if you have a family and children, there is only so much limiting you can do... again, duty first.

Your environment will either be conducive to distractions or cultivated with discipline.

5. Be More Firm Than Flexible

You teach people how to treat you. With all the varying personalities in the world with their respective nuances and idiosyncrasies, how else will they learn? For instance, a person will not learn to not call you after 9 pm if you continue to answer the phone or refuse to tell them. A person will not learn to not take your kindness for weakness if you always behave as a milquetoast. Oftentimes, people do not mean any harm; they simply do not know. Therefore, it is okay to convey your standards and boundaries in a way that would be received and understood—tactfully and *firmly*. Most people know how to read between the lines, but for those who don't, kindly teach them and tell them how. And when it comes to self-discipline and training yourself for effectiveness, remain firm and consistent.

News Flash...

Your poor planning does not constitute an emergency or distraction for me.

Four Simple Ways to Eliminate Distractions

If you do not prioritize your work, you won't get anything done.

1. Declutter
- Get rid of the mess and drama.
- Get organized.
- Gather your thoughts.

2. Determine, Define, and Decide Early On
- Schedule, strategize, plan ahead, set deadlines and due dates, make to-do and task lists, establish a game plan, and automate what you can (e.g., paying your bills, calendar reminders). Take advantage of technology in a good way.
- Set boundaries, limits, and standards (be firm about what you will and won't tolerate) and follow through without compromise.
- *Determine* what is within your locus of control, and *decide* how, when, and what you need to carry it out. Deciding (planning) early helps you to get "in the flow" of things while limiting distractions and positioning you to work in tandem with your goals and dreams. Create visual management (e.g., make vision boards, write down *defined and determined* goals... targets, baselines, and benchmarks; check off as you achieve them).

A dream sought-after is merely a wish,
until it's written and worked as a goal.

Invest in tools, tasks and technology that will save you time.

FOCUS = right *frame of mind*, right *framework*
SUCCESS = right *structure*, right *systems*, right *schedule*, right *self-concept*

Disciplined decision-making is essential to limiting and eliminating distractions.

3. **Delegate** - Seek help; lean on the support of others; assign tedious tasks to someone who can assist with accomplishing them; hire a virtual assistant—www.vrproassistant.com.

4. **Discuss/Defuse** - Get an accountability partner and discuss your goals and plans. Resolve issues, conflicts, and problems; confront matters that contribute to external disruptions and internal distractions to render a solution (e.g., see a doctor, seek therapy, engage in conflict resolution and mediation, have those difficult conversations, reconcile with family and friends, pray/confess, etc.) Oftentimes, to conquer you must confront when necessary, but remember to do so humbly and honestly.

*Don't miss your moment for a
moment's distraction.*

"To each there comes in their lifetime a special moment when they are figuratively tapped on the shoulder and offered the chance to do a very special thing, unique to them and fitted to their talents. What a tragedy if that moment finds them unprepared or unqualified for that which could have been their finest hour."

— Winston Churchill

Chapter 3

15 Distractions Aimed to Deter and Discourage

1. Daily Tasks and Trifles

E mails, phone calls, text messages, questions, requests, solicitations, social media, traffic, bills, breaking news, rumors, threats, accidents, people/relationships — their respective feelings, emotions, idiosyncrasies and the list goes on and on. Everyday life can be overwhelming; however, you cannot give daily life carte blanche to do whatever it wants to do. You cannot allow daily life to walk over your authority, diminish your power, and distract ad nauseum.

The vicissitudes and demands of life are in and of themselves one big distraction. We've all heard the cliché truisms, "change is inevitable"; "some things are just out of your control." No matter how hackneyed, these statements are profoundly true. The key is not to focus on what we cannot control but on the things we can control. The majority of the daily distractions you experience are within your control. For example, it is within your control to not watch five hours of TV a day. It is within your control to not read every email, answer every call, respond to every text, fulfill every favor, bow to every emotion, and appease every asking at a moment's notice.

Oftentimes, when you respond hastily, you hinder current focus, become off-kilter, and juggle too many things at once. Doing this changes the trajectory of your day and spills over into the week, and even the months ahead, resulting in delays and unnecessary nothingness.

2. **Debt/Dollars**

Debt is one of the biggest distractions. With the national U.S. debt in the trillions of dollars, individual (consumer) debt is also a mammoth mass when you consider the debt-to-income ratio. Consequently, people are distracted by their bondage of bills and work tirelessly to pay bills or pay them off entirely with hopes of becoming debt-free. Credit card debt, student loan debt, mortgage/rent, car payments, standard monthly bills, and loans overall can exasperate anxiety and limit focus. The more debt you have and the less you can pay, the more distracting debt is. And to the contrary, the more you pay down and pay off while maintaining a decent income, the less distracting debt becomes and the more freedom you feel.

Paying bills may seem like a duty; however, do not be deceived. Debt and bills are no duty. They are your responsibility because they are debts that you created and therefore must pay. Distractions, like debt, take away; they subtract from your life, often reducing your overall net worth—but only from an economic standpoint because your inherent worth is priceless.

Additionally, mismanaging finances and compounding debt undoubtedly subtract from your peace of mind and increase the amount of money you spend on bills, interest, penalties, and fees, thus reducing your discretionary income.

Debt is a thief; it steals your time, energy, peace, and joy which blurs your vision and focus. Debt robs you of your creativity and assaults your capability. You are a talented and gifted individual, but oftentimes these gifts and talents lie dormant because distractions run amok unfettered and unhindered. When you are worried about debt, and work countless hours to pay bills, this distracts you from your purpose, your destiny, and limits your creative potential. There may be times when you want to step out (i.e., start a new business and invest in your ideas), but you have mountains of debt that you cannot seem to climb out from under. You are walking on a thin tightrope where one mistake, one missed payment, one missed paycheck, could make regaining your balance almost impossible, thus sending you down into the abyss of financial ruin. The negative emotions that debt brings—stress, pressure, fear, depression, and anxiety are the essence of debt's powerful ability to distract, deter and discourage.

Conversely, there may be instances when you are not pressured for money, but your impulsive desire to make more money and impetuously spend on material things for the purposes of keeping up, showing off, fitting in, or just to feel better about yourself can also become a frivolous distraction. Many psychologists believe that the amount of money people earn is significantly linked to how they feel about themselves. There are many people who allow their net-worth to dictate their self-worth; they allow money to determine the value and meaning of their lives. Money does not make your life more valuable, but what you do with your life and what you do for others engenders meaning and significance. Chasing dollars... chasing money outside of providing for the needs of your family, and working two to three jobs, plus a side gig, can be your hustle but could be diminishing the mental and emotional muscle it takes for you to be truly productive and live a purpose-filled life.

What are your core values? What exactly are you trying to achieve... freedom, autonomy, peace of mind, generational wealth, or a lasting legacy? Without sacrificing what really matters, allow your values to be your fuel (your drive) and not necessarily the value of money. Don't allow trade-offs to make you a trader to your duties—find a healthy balance. Love yourself, pursue your dreams but love others too, and influence their reality. Understand that being interrupted or inconvenienced to fulfill a duty or to really help someone, whether it is with your money, knowledge (expertise) or time, is not a definite distraction, no matter how counterproductive it may seem. We are all called to help and serve others. Steward your money and time wisely, but never be stingy with it or with helping others.

"We live in the day of distractomania, but you can find something, some life that you touched, something that you did that made the doing worthwhile."— Mary Crowley

Moreover, to effectively operate within your sphere of influence, limited time, and resources, you must lean on *discernment* and divine direction because you cannot help everyone, nor are you meant to. The key point here is that *you were born for others and not for yourself, so make the best use of your time as you live your life and help (love) others.* This truth is evident when we consider the impact that our lives have on others from a micro and macro-level standpoint. For instance, your decisions do not just impact you. *Your choices do not relegate consequences to you alone—but those around you are also affected by the consequences of your choices.* **Your aim should never be self-centeredness.**

Irrespective of your financial state, whether plentiful or pitiful, what are you doing to impact the lives of others? *Some things are worth more than dollars, and you can never put a price on purpose and peace.*

Perspective is paramount. When you believe in yourself and view yourself as already rich in morals, values, and faith as a unique, capable, and productive individual, this will in turn feed your self-esteem, self-worth, and self-confidence. There is no one on the planet like you who has been gifted to do what you can do. I believe the following two points are essential to generating meaningful and material success.

- You must *prep for profit and progress* by learning, growing, and connecting. Opportunities are always available, but are you ready to embrace them without the distractions?

- *Personal evolution precedes personal earnings.* Allow personal growth to be your aim and the personal gems (money/success) will follow. Remember, it is not about what you have, but who you are and who you become.

Additionally, being indebted to others, or feeling like you owe someone for their help, gifts or favors, or someone making you feel like you owe them are also mentally distracting. Some people manipulate situations and do things for others because they want something in return or want to try to control you. Their whole motive is wrong, and they do things with ill intentions. Bribes, quid pro quo "this for that", and other forms of manipulation all fall within this category. Life is hard enough without someone holding you over a barrel. Of course, if you owe someone pursuant to a valid agreement or contract, then do your due diligence to pay them back and make good on your promise.

3. **Deficiency** - Deficiencies can operate in the form of insecurities, insufficiencies, impairments, inadequacies and inabilities. The "I cant's" become the distraction that inactivates and malfunctions your internal wire of success. Deficiencies are debilitating because they short-circuit the self-image and positive thinking which inevitably affects behavior negatively. The rudimentary

lessons that we learned early in life are essentially relevant—'If you think you can't, you won't. If you think you can, you will.' *"As a man thinks so is he."* [1] So try to maintain a positive outlook; don't listen to the negative distracting voices around you (including your own).

Moreover, a deficiency does not necessarily equate to a definite deficit; it only means you must humbly depend on and plug into another power source to turn up the greatness within you. For instance, God's strength is made perfect in weakness when you rely on this primary power source and fountainhead of faith. His grace is sufficient.

Insecure people make themselves the target of torment and terror because they focus on themselves. Shift your focus from self-defeating and self-deprecating mindsets and thinking.

Additionally, deficiencies can also come in the form of voids in our heart and brokenness in our soul. Rejection, abandonment, lack, and neglect build blocks of deficiencies on the foundation of our hearts, creating an insecure person who can collapse at any moment. People then feverishly work to protect, prove, defend, hide, impress, and fit in to cover and fill the voids. Comparison, competitiveness, and covetousness then creep into the crevices of the heart because the person feels that they are deficient in certain areas. Jealousy and envy then clog up the soul, creating a distracted and divided mind with thoughts of somebody having more and doing more.

As a result, many push, pull, and perform to be better and do better while denying their authentic self (calling and destiny). Filter out envy, jealousy, fear, and self-defeating stinky thinking.

"To be content doesn't mean you don't desire more, it means you are thankful for what you have and patient for what's to come." – Tony Gaskins

Contentment and *faith* are the secrets to mitigating internal distractions and living a purpose-filled, peaceful life.

"Faith gives you an inner strength and a sense of balance and perspective in life." – Gregory Peck

Note: A time *deficiency* could also be a distraction trigger. Leaving late, running late and poor planning can disrupt your mental mood.

4. **Deliberations/Debates/Disputes/ Discussions** – Futile arguments, constant back and forth, gossip, rumors, lies, slander, playing the blame game (finger pointing and faultfinding), politicizing, misunderstandings, pontificating, excessive complaining, criticizing, nagging, accusations, unresolved conflict, filibusters, propaganda, and unrelenting communication with someone with itchy ears, a closed mind, and a hard heart are all distractions that fuel emotions and fractures focus.

"Rumors are dainty morsels that sink deep into one's heart." [2]

And let's not forget about those who seemingly lose a debate or dispute. How many times have you mulled over what you should have said, what you did not say, and what you wish you could take back? How distracting is that?

So what is all the fuss really about (motive and intent)? What or who can be potentially gained from the debate or discussion? Is it worth it? Will the dispute foster change for the greater good or will it only flame quarrels and strife? These are all questions one must answer when deciding to engage in deliberations, debates, discussions, and disputes. To be silent is to be in agreement and indifferent towards change; and to speak without bringing value, substance, or edification is to be an accessory to futility. Your highest goal in life should be love and unity, not to win arguments.

Wisdom and discernment provide the perfect balance between not speaking and knowing when to.

In the words of the wise, when trying to win over someone for their benefit and best interest, don't just answer their question but humbly reach the person behind the question; "don't lose the person while trying to win the argument"; and "listen first to understand and then to be understood" (Stephen Covey). And when stating your case, present the facts in a civil manner; try to avoid raising your voice and displaying anger. I know that it's easy to get caught up in the heat of the moment and difficult to refrain from becoming visibly upset when you or someone you care about are being verbally attacked or accused. But always try to maintain your grip and keep a tight lid on your emotions to maintain a firm footing. Let go, forgive, and move forward.

"Meekness is not weakness. It is strength under control." – Unknown

5. **Disease** – With the recent COVID-19 pandemic, we realize now more than ever before how one sickness can become one virally vast distraction. So can any disease for that matter, no matter how acute or chronic, short-term or long-term, treatable or non-curable. For instance, a headache (whether a symptom of a disease or triggered by tension), may seem trivial, but if it hurts bad enough, it could undoubtedly distract you from your day. Notice 'Dis'-ease, a separation from being at ease. Prayer, rest, proper nutrition, exercise, medicine, meditation, and the support of doctors, family, and friends all help to reconnect you with 'ease.'

6. **Disorders/Disabilities** – Some diseases may result in long-term disorders and lifelong disabilities. And because of the emotional and mental toll this can have on a person's psyche, it could accelerate a mass distraction of *depression* for the long-haul. I think about Helen Keller, who was both blind and deaf, yet she did not allow these disabilities to distract her from fulfilling her dreams. Despite her shortcomings, she was the first blind-deaf person to earn a bachelor's degree and was an avid writer and speaker. She relentlessly advocated for people with disabilities, handicaps, and limitations. She believed in herself and others

no matter their disorder or disability. In the same manner, believe in yourself, and trust that when a weakness develops, a strength steps up to engender perfect synergy.

Moreover, mental disorders such as depression and psychosis are linked to many distractions of life which is why it is so important to protect yourself from unnecessary stress—the distractions and demands of this world. Juggling too much could lead to a mental, emotional, or nervous breakdown.

7. **Disparity** – Actions of injustice, microaggression, economic disadvantage, inequality, prejudices, partiality, implicit and institutional bias, gender bias, infringement of rights, disenfranchisement, disproportionate impact, underrepresentation, segregation, and discrimination can instantly take you off focus, triggering anger, offense, hostility, resentment, bitterness, discouragement, anxiety, and frustration. It is important to note, however, some things that appear to be distractions are signs to direct you to a greater duty (e.g., stand up for what's right, advocate for others, etc.).

8. **Doubt/Dread/Distress/Desperation** – Doubt (double-mindedness) and dread are rooted in uncertainty and fear. Have you ever considered that your distractions could be the manifestation of your fears (e.g., fear of failure, fear of rejection, fear of being talked about, fear of being hurt, fear of commitment)? Oftentimes, your fears become internal distractions within themselves, and as a

result you may deliberately yield to external distractions because you are afraid of leaving your comfort zone and doing the things you know you should do. You allow distractions to become excuses—the scapegoat for unproductivity.

Therefore, when we choose not to move forward because of worry and fear, we *allow* ourselves to be distracted—complicit in stagnation which results in procrastination, postponement, and poor planning. Be real with yourself. Rid yourself of distractions, step out on faith and make it happen. Don't allow your fears to hide behind the distractions you tolerate. "Avoidance behavior" is the biggest cop-out.

"The greatest enemy of success is your fear of failure"
- Unknown

Moreover, if you dread fulfilling a request, communicating with others, attending a job interview, speaking in front of people, going to the doctor, or completing a task, this will distract you not only from doing the things you have committed to do and need to do, but could also mentally distract you from other daily tasks and responsibilities. Doubt and dread can result in frustration, discouragement, and mental anguish. After doubt pulls the plug on positivity, dread kills the light of external enthusiasm. Sometimes, the tasks are not as bad as we *think* they are, it all stems from the mind—the imagination. In my dreadful experiences, when the task(s) is finally done, I'd often say to myself in relief, "It wasn't that bad," and many times it isn't. And in other instances, I misjudged the entire situation. I perceived it or the person totally wrong. Negative emotions, discouragement, and despair (internal distractions and barriers) could disrupt your will to overcome (willpower) and leave you stuck where you are—unable to focus and move forward.

One day, I was wallowing in self-pity over an issue that seemed too formidable for me to overcome. I stopped and said to myself, "Stop it! What you focus on you magnify, and what you magnify, you manifest." This was profound, and ever so true. Sometimes what we fear and dread the most comes upon us because we believe and have more faith in the things we fear. It's time to shift your focus with a good attitude and have faith for good things—for positive, productive and meaningful change. Doubt often stops you from trying and striving, and dread dulls the moment.

"Doubt kills more dreams than failure ever will." - Suzy Kassem

Furthermore, *desperation* magnetizes itself to doubt. The difference between the two is that doubt is often passive-aggressive, and desperation is more aggressive. For instance, I may doubt that I won't get the job, but when I am desperate, I may constantly call to follow-up on the application, send emails and may even show up at the employer's office to express my overwhelming interest. The desperation was triggered by the doubt. Doubt and desperation (despair/hopelessness) are the primary culprits for many comorbid conditions such as depression, stress, substance abuse, suicidal ideation, and other health issues.

9. **Dysfunction** – Dysfunction can come in the form of strife, jealousy, dissention, distrust, infighting, incivility, disruption, chaos, breakdowns, betrayals, obsession, negative thinking, internalized anger, delusions, self-denial (refusing to take responsibility or acknowledge a problem), self-pity, false sense of responsibility, emotional instability, and exaggerated problems. Relational dysfunction, familial dysfunction, emotional dysfunction, and mental dysfunction often collide creating an avalanche of disorder and confusion of every kind. Dysfunction can reside in the heart (the mind), home, workplace, within politics, schools, and even in the church. As we learned earlier, 'dys'-function separates you from normal function. Activities and circumstances that bring discontent and dysfunction will result in a person being afraid, insecure, and immensely distracted. Hence, dysfunctional environments fraught with abuse, hate, malice, hostility, intimidation, confusion, negativity, and drama will lead to poor performance, increased anxiety, mental and emotional turmoil, unproductivity, and lack of focus.

Dysfunction is one distraction that must be addressed quickly to stop it from taking up indefinite domain. If dysfunction goes unreproved and unopposed, its poison will inhibit growth, progression, and good health. The toxicity, mental distress and frustration that comes with dysfunction disables the function of your focus.

10. **Death and Devastation** - Sudden, massive, and excessive loss is the common denominator with death and devastation. Death is something that is certain to happen at some point in our lives, yet many are unprepared spiritually and financially (e.g., no life insurance*) which results in a bigger distraction for the family left behind. Death is imminent and immutable, and the fear of it happening or to experience the death of a loved one destabilizes the soul and motions the mind to worry, wonder, and wander as it grieves. Devastation is sudden, intense, traumatic, heart-pounding (heart breaking), earth-shattering, and jaw dropping; it can come in many ways, such as loss of a loved one, job loss, financial loss, divorce, breakups, betrayals, accidents, sickness/unfavorable diagnosis, violence, natural disasters, wars, etc. In a moment of loss and grief, one must yield to this distraction to allow the process of healing and resilience to begin.

*Learn more about the benefits and types of life insurance at www.fflifeinsurance.com.

11. **Drama** - There is so much drama in the world today where every single second seems like a live theatrical performance or motion-pictured movie. I mean, the

stuff that we see and hear, you just cannot make up. It's inconceivable, incomprehensible, unbelievable, unimaginable, unexplainable, unconscionable, and insurmountable—drastic drama! I've learned that some people just love drama; they invent and manufacture drama for days on end and can't wait to tell you all about it. Their drama, infused with negativity, naivete, and narcissism, could ruin your entire day, even if you only listen to a minute of it. One minute of drama can become one day of annoyance and a moment's distraction. If you want to rid yourself of distractions, you must *dismiss* and *disarm the drama*. Drama free is the best way to be! It's true that drama and sensationalism sells, but if you are not buying or getting paid to listen to it or deal with the drama, why entertain it? Why waste your time? Unless you like it too. Don't be a drama queen or king, or one that rolls out the red carpet for drama distractors and deliverers to stroll down the aisle to the doorway of your life... ready to dump their drama junk full of gossip and negativity.

12. **Devices** - I know you've heard this countless times, but devices unsupervised and unrestrained can undoubtedly be a distraction. Like anything, "a good thing can become a bad thing, if it becomes the main thing." Technology in and of itself is not bad; it is how you use technology and how long you use it that can pose a problem. With the proliferation of technology, devices have caused a major disruption on our roads, in our relationships, in the classrooms, and at the dinner table. People are worried over who liked their post, who friended and unfriended them,

and who followed and unfollowed them. They are concerned with quantity—the number of likes and friends, instead of the quality of their lives. Texts, posts, tweets, responses, and replies have become a pseudo emergency that demands your immediate attention only to steal your focus from what really matters. Carve out time for technology use; like anything, consider putting it on a schedule. And don't get too caught up in the world wide web—social media and the internet, or you could become entangled in the web of distraction and injected with its toxic virtual venom. And never allow technology to command your morning by letting it be the first thing you do, unless it aids in meditation, prayer, affirmation, and positive thinking.

13. **Disappointments** – Betrayals, break ups, breakdowns, let downs, fall outs, divorce, rejection, lack of support, false promises, missed opportunities, unmet expectations, unwise choices, mistakes, failed relationships, financial setbacks, layoffs, terminations, business failure, personal failure, health failure (unfavorable prognosis and diagnosis), bad test results, bad news, lawsuits, afflictions, attacks, hardships, opposition, defeat, loss, unanswered (delayed) prayers, unforeseen circumstances, disapproval, and the list of disappointments goes on and on. Like most distractions, disappointments are inevitable; they are a part of life. Remember, you have resilient resolve. *Believe* for the best, *break free*, and *bounce back* from the disappointments of life with faith, fortitude, and fervor.

14. **Desires** - Wrong desires, and even an obsession with some right desires, can distract you from what really matters. Addictions, cravings, urges, compulsions, impulses, envy, jealousy, covetousness, unnecessary comparison, materialism, greed, bad habits, egomania, pride, the need to control, debauchery, lusts, longings, and the "paralysis of analysis," a.k.a. 'perfectionism', can all build up as piles of distractions. Wanting what someone else has can distract you from what you do have; counting your problems and desiring immediate solutions will discount your blessings; indulging in bad habits will keep you from establishing good habits; desiring what is wrong will distract you from desiring what is right; trying to control everything and everyone is mentally and emotionally exhausting and is indicative of a control freak.

Our desires are perpetuated by our problems or something we lack. The very essence of our desires stem from a problem or a perceived problem. When the current outcome is different from the desired state, this creates a *desire* longed for and sought after. Henry David Thoreau refers to this as "quiet desperation." Longings can lull you into an emotional whirlwind—and what you seek after and long for could lead you the wrong way as you chase after the wrong things or things that should have less priority.

Essentially, giving in to distractions is giving up what really matters for a moment's desire. What are you giving up when you give in to distractions for a moment's desire? Is it your time, your family, your friends, your dream, your freedom, your character and integrity, your life, your inheritance? I recall a biblical story about a man (Esau) who gave up his birthright (his inheritance) because he was hungry and *desired* a pot of stew, so he exchanged his birthright for it. Are you giving up what is valuable and long-term for what is temporary and short-lived? Are you giving up what is fleeting and perishable for what can have a meaningful impact and lasting legacy?

If you get too hung up on the desire or distraction, you could miss what's right in front of you.

My greatest regret in life was not fully enjoying my son when he was a young child and seizing every precious moment. I was so caught up in my pain and what I wanted that I missed the beautiful gift that was right in front of me. Don't become blind to the blessings in your life because you are too focused on your desires—what you want and what you think you need.

15. **Decisions** – Life is full of decisions (choices) that result in bad decisions, good decisions, and 'only time will tell' decisions. Indecisiveness, dilemmas, quandaries, "right vs. right and right vs. wrong paradigms,"[5] contemplations and weighing the benefits against the risks all involve a decision that must be made. Spending a lot of time mulling over a decision and wallowing in acute ambivalence, cognitive dissonance, and regret after making a decision—doubting and second-guessing yourself—can be mentally exhausting. "If only I had done this; if only I had done that," reverberates incessantly in your mind and leads to more distractions crammed with disappointment, discouragement, and dysfunction. Not being sure what to decide or what will be the best choice can become nerve-wracking as it shakes and shifts your focus. Don't overthink it; weigh your options; pray about it; seek wise counsel; do what's right; unselfishly consider the greater good (other people); do sufficient research; evaluate the pros, cons and the benefits against the risks; sleep on it; hope for the best; believe in yourself, forgive yourself (and others); and be confident.

Rushworth M. Kidder stated: *"Those who live in close proximity to their basic values are apt to agonize over choices that other people, drifting over the surface of their lives, might never even see as problems. Sound values raise tough choices; and tough choices are never easy."* [3]

Additionally, with the proliferation of information, mostly searched and discovered on the internet, deciding what to buy and who to buy it from, who to follow, who to recruit, who to hire, who to date, who to trust, who to listen to, who to watch, who to contact, who, who, who... can become daunting and overwhelming. Simply settle down and regroup to reduce the friction of your focus.

*Essentially, your decisions should
get you closer to your aim.*

Another distraction around decision-making involves people who try to control your *decisions*... wanting it their way or no way. Living out someone else's written script for your life diminishes your power and purpose as a unique individual in your own life's story. Never allow someone to run your life by binding their decisions, dreams, demands, and desires to you. I am not saying you should rebel, or not be receptive to wise counsel, constructive criticism, helpful feedback or sound principles and policies. I am simply saying not to be ruled by other peoples' expectations, opinions, and approval.

*Regardless of your decisions, good or bad, learn from
them and aim to make better decisions in the future.*

Distractions are inseparable from life; they are inescapable. Like different stages and seasons of life, distractions will come in the form of problems, predicaments, and pain. It is not because these distractions are aiming for you or singled you out, and it is not because a cosmic force put a hit out on you—it is because we live in a fallen world that aims for all of us, no matter your age, race, ethnicity, gender, or religious affiliation. Distractions do not discriminate. Some distractions, however, are the harvest of what was sown, such as poor planning, disorganization, procrastination, neglect of duties and responsibilities. But regardless, when the distractions of life happen and hit you hard, you must choose to deal with them, rise above them or be defeated. As the popular saying goes, "When life gives you lemons, make lemonade." Or, in other words, when life throws you a curve ball, catch it and throw it back straight. Don't bend to the curve but learn from the curve to perfect your aim and hit new targets.

Make the most of every opportunity (convert problems into opportunities).

Most problems we encounter come with an opportunity for gain and growth—a level of convertibility, but you must be wise enough to recognize it and learn from the premise of the problem and the detriment of the distraction.

And, to the contrary, oftentimes opportunities are full of possibilities but could become a problem if not handled wisely. *Therefore, be careful not to pursue and yield to every opportunity and every possibility because this too can become a distraction and a burden. Everything that looks good, is not good, or is not good for you. When you narrow your focus and zoom in on your niche, you can achieve much more.*

Daily disciplines prepare you for rare opportunities.

In a nutshell, the secret to defeating distractions is to recognize them for what they are—to see past the surface and be wary of the pitfalls that are aimed to trip you up and derail your destiny.

Chapter 4

Destiny Disruptors

Destiny is predetermined purpose and the fulfillment of divine moments that are aligned with the trajectory of that purpose to achieve God's overall plan for your life.

D istractions are destiny disruptors. Therefore, don't become so distracted by stuff that it keeps you from moving forward into your destiny. Know when to stop, leave, and walk away. Situations and people become disruptors when they dismiss your dream, limit your focus, and hinder your growth.

Use your time wisely. And remember, the process to your dreams, desires and destiny may take time, but it will be worth it in the end, if you stay the course and don't get sidetracked by the distractions of life. **Find your flow and go with the flow as you work to juggle your duties while managing the distractions.** Forfend your focus and defend your duties by limiting disruptions and eliminating distractions within your span of control.

No one is impervious to distractions, but everyone has the power to manage distractions effectively.

However, sometimes when managing distractions, one might unwittingly perceive a duty as a distraction. When you view a duty as a disrupter (a nuisance) those around you will know it because it will be reflected in your actions and attitude. For example, viewing parenting as a distraction will show up in your behavior and disposition. Kids will sense the indifference and may feel unloved and unwanted as a result. Put duties and distractions in their proper place. Honor duties delightfully with a heart of servitude built on a foundation of love. View duties as honorable and not as a distraction. Marriages and other key relationships will flourish when you do this. Remember, no one wants to be tolerated, but everyone wants to be celebrated and feel like they matter.

All actions are not distractions, but distractions can stifle the actions that really matter.

Tactical Tip: When juggling duties such as spending time with family and aiming for your personal and professional goals, continuously communicate with your family (i.e., spouse/kids) to get them on board and to gain their buy-in and support within reason. Make hitting your goals an exciting play for the entire family where the outcomes of achieving your goals benefit them as well in a meaningful way. Remember, *greedy* goals are selfish (benefits you only), *gutsy* goals are ambitious, and *Godly* goals are faith-filled.

Greatness knows no bound.
Living out your purpose transcends your posterity.

Dormant Distractions

We've discussed the top 15 distractions that are easily detectable. But what about the distractions that lie secretly, subtly, and stagnantly beneath the surface of the heart. *Dormant distractions* are impalpable disruptors that are rooted deep within the recesses of your mind, or your subconscious, sometimes unknowingly to you. These distractions germinate within the soul and often manifest themselves in the form of insidious dreams (nightmares), discouragement, depression, despair, and distress. Although these distractions are deceptively dormant, they operate through the unconscious mind and hinder progress.

Dormant distractions commonly involve: suppressed pain, repressed memories, unresolved anger, nagging feelings, offenses, past hurts, adverse childhood experiences, mental exhaustion, fear, anxiety, dread, unanswered questions, unforgiveness, wrong perceptions and assumptions, insecurities, low self-esteem, inner conflict/barriers, negative mindsets and attitudes, unconscious or limiting beliefs, guilt, unmet expectations, and eviscerated potential, which are all subtle, crafty, and rooted deep within a person's psyche. Things that you regret, resent and relish... things that you know you should be doing, or things you know you should not be doing... things that you should have done, or not done, can all distract your internal operating system.

To rid yourself of dormant distractions—the emotional enchantments and entanglements (the invisible, internal, and intangible distractions that you can't easily cut off, control, or ignore), you must confront them head on with courage, honesty, forgiveness, and professional help, as necessary.

Many people make *decisions* based on dormant distractions that have no basis in reality but sadly they shape their reality. Here is a tactical tip: If you know the origin (the root) of the internal distractions that lie dormant within your soul, you have the advantage and the ability to destroy what you cannot see.

It is your duty to rid yourself of anything that holds you back and holds you bound.

One personal example of a dormant distraction is when I neglected for years to get on the treadmill at home. I always thought I was just being lazy and resistant to exercise, but subconsciously my will had been deactivated and debilitated by a dormant distraction. Initially, the treadmill was upstairs in my husband's man cave. Therefore, to keep from disturbing him and him disturbing me, I only wanted to get on the treadmill when he was not at home. But since he spends 90% of his time in the "man cave" and we work similar schedules, it was difficult to find an ideal time to work out. My husband never told me or acted as if I was bothering him, but for some reason in the back of my mind (dormant distraction), I felt that I did. And he never really bothered me (except for the time when he sneaked behind me and slapped me on the butt while I was walking on the treadmill).

I thought that he would repeat his facetious deeds again and again (eventually causing me to fall on my face), so I came up with excuses in my mind and never really established them as distractions to be dealt with. One day, I thought, "What if I moved the treadmill downstairs to another room... maybe I would use it more." I did, and the distractions and excuses were moved right along with it— they completely diminished. I now get on the treadmill almost every day versus less than 20 times a year, because I eradicated the dormant distractions from my mind. Oftentimes, the intensity of our imaginations and the fruitfulness of our fears inhibit the consideration of viable and simple solutions.

The mind is the greatest distraction.
Dormant distractions often dominate and dictate.

Consequently, our duties can also become dormant distractions when our roles with their varying personalities conflict. For instance, a wife, mother, and boss—one person with three different roles, could have internal conflict when these roles and their respective duties collide or when one vies for more time. Or as Michael Gerber points out, the roles and business personalities of an entrepreneur (one person, three roles) often conflict with each other's aim and hinder small business success. These conflicting roles are: (1) Technician (doer, thinker), (2) Manager (planner, organizer) and (3) Entrepreneur (visionary, innovator).[1]

Additionally, there is the inner conflict (distraction) with becoming who you're called to be and doing what you're called to do which often fights with your old self (thinking/mindsets, desires, insecurities, inhibitions, attitudes and behaviors). Similarly, the good conscience competing and combating with the bad conscience. To remedy this, identify your core purpose, values, virtues, and primary identity, and work around that. This may mean delegating duties, hiring help, giving up bad habits, renewing your mind (changing the way you think), and yielding to your calling to embrace and support who you really are.

Fatal Distraction Attractions

Getting caught up in the hustle and bustle of life is one of the most infamous distractions. *For many, distractions are a form of intentional escapism that drags people away willingly from their duties and responsibilities.*

Fatal distraction attractions kill your focus, time, energy, and enthusiasm. They kidnap your soul (mind, will and emotions) and smother your potential.

Violating and neglecting duties are signs of *fatal distraction attractions.* To combat this, filter your focus and flush out the senseless and superfluous tasks, excuses, requests and thinking. You do this by realigning your actions with your duties and goals; and as you self-correct you'll resurrect your ability to achieve with an ardent aim.

Wrong and unbalanced desires often kill devotion and duty—which could ultimately result in a real-life disaster.

Choose not to be a silent partner with distractions; instead, be a viable opponent who not only rejects unnecessary distractions, but refrains from becoming a distractor (e.g., backstabber, bully, busybody, deceiver, gossiper, hater, rebel, saboteur, trickster, troublemaker, tyrant, malefactor, manipulator, or meddler). The world has enough distractions, so don't become one.

Find your place, find your purpose, and make the world and your sphere of influence better because of you. Contrary to popular opinion, which is sensationalized via TV and other mediums, confusion, drama and disorder are not attractive; they only precipitate *fatal distraction attractions.*

Distractions are the enemy of purpose, progress, productivity, and profitability.

Rather than allowing distractions to kill your time and talents, *gain* the upper hand—and *kill and crush your dreams and goals by achieving them.*

Six Simple Ways to Achieve Your Dreams

1. *Set* your mind to achieve (believe in yourself; fill your mind with knowledge, constructive thoughts, and intrinsic motivation; focus on the positive and fend off the negative)
2. *Structure* your day (what will you do)
3. *Strategize* (how will you do it)
4. *Schedule* (when will you do it)
5. *Sacrifice* (what will you give up to do it) Hint: Give up distractions and make wise tradeoffs.
6. *Step out* on faith... overcome fear and make it happen.

Relax and Distract

Distractions have their place; we cannot engage in duties 24/7 and fully divest or deprive ourselves of distractions. Hence, the objective is not to encourage you to become a full-fledged, full-time "distraction deputy sheriff"—arresting and restraining every distraction that comes your way. Rather, this book aims to prepare you for "guard *duty*" and supply you with enough ammunition to curtail the power of distractions. The key is to keep distractions in their proper place and not allow them to dominate your time or hijack your attention for an indefinite period. Similarly to planning and prioritizing your day, grant yourself permission to plan a time to be reasonably distracted within the confines of your relaxation time, or periods when you choose to make an extemporaneous exception for a brief break.

To support a healthy equilibrium, schedule downtime by carving out time to relax and unplug. Relaxing activities or "brain breaks" may include engaging in hobbies, enjoying life, reading, sitting in solitude, watching a good movie, vacationing, exhaling from a stressful day, and entertaining distractions within good reason.

However, keep in mind, only distractions that are appropriate, reasonable, and safe, should be considered worthy of your time—of course, in their proper place (positionally in terms of prioritization and physically as it relates to the place in which the distraction occurs). For instance, you wouldn't play a game of solitaire on your phone while driving a car (inappropriate place, unsafe, and unreasonable), and you would not binge watch TV when you know you should be studying for a test tomorrow (poor prioritization). In a nutshell, proper planning, prioritization, productivity, passionate pursuits, positive thinking, periods of enjoyment, and purpose-filled actions all make life worthwhile.

Work-life balance and brief breaks are essential to maintaining a high level of performance and productivity.

Chapter 5

Wanderer, Swanderer, Squanderer, Aimer

When it comes to distractions, essentially there are four types of people:

1. **Wanderer** - The nomadic "wanderer" is slowly walking on the treadmill of life. He has a target (a sense of a duty or two) but there's really no definitive targets or goals with any real color or texture; and no sense of urgency to make anything happen. His mind wonders as he wanders through life aimlessly with an indifferent attitude.

A sense of urgency is a unilateral awareness that could have a utilitarian effect. The time is now for productive change!

2. **Swanderer** - The "swanderer" is a purposeful wanderer. Her final destination is known, but she does other sporadic things as she moves through life. She is running on the treadmill of life reaching for targets—duties and dreams, but she won't get off the treadmill long enough to aim and hit her targets successfully. She is so busy and distracted that she unwittingly smirks at the wanderers and squanderers. "What in the world," she says as she watches them walk slowly and backward on the treadmill of life. However, she does not realize that she is no better because although she is running, reaching and multi-tasking, she is not hitting her targets. She has targets, she has dreams, she is aware of her duties, but she is missing the mark because she won't make time to nail her target(s).

3. **Squanderer** - The "squanderer" is in a state of oblivion. He is uncertain about his very existence—his purpose. He is so confused about where he is going, and what he truly wants that he walks backward on the treadmill of life. He has no targets, only a blank board with no perceived duties or dreams. He squanders away his time and talents and stumbles as he walks and runs the wrong way, oftentimes tripping over his insolent pride.

Squanderer
"Oblivion"

"I got this! Oops"...he stumbles.

4. **Aimer** - The "aimer" knows what she wants and where she is going. She keeps it moving and can manage duties, responsibilities, and distractions well. She does what needs to be done and gets off the treadmill of life (working and dealing with distractions) to focus and aim at hitting targets—her duties and dreams.

Aimer

Which one are you? _____

Change has two sides of the same coin; sometimes it is the head and out of your control, and other times it is the tail and waits on you to make it happen.

Tactical Tips:

- Productivity is about getting things done—making incremental increases, gradual gains, small steps, and large leaps (double duty), when necessary, to achieve your goal. Just think if you committed 30 minutes or more a day to a specific task, project, or goal such as writing or reading a book, studying, exercising, or completing chores. Think about how much you could get done over time. Either you will allow the darts of distractions to target you, knock you down and burn you out, or you will dodge distractions, stop, focus, and aim to hit your targets (duties and dreams).

  Helen Keller stated, *"I long to accomplish a great and noble task, but it is my chief duty to accomplish small tasks as if they were great and noble."*

- Try to focus on one task at a time. It takes longer to complete tasks when multi-tasking (doing more than one thing at once) versus tackling tasks one project at a time. However, when multi-tasking is necessary, focus your mind on the task at hand instead of thinking about all the other things you must do. The secret is to have a laser-like focus on the activity you are doing at that very moment. This will give you the greatest expenditure of your time. Additionally, note that even mindless tasks require a certain level of focus. For instance, I can wash dishes and watch TV simultaneously; although washing dishes does not require much mental effort,

I could probably complete the task much quicker and have cleaner dishes if I were not watching TV.

- When juggling multiple tasks, projects and businesses, delegate days to maximize your time, focus and effort. For example, on Mondays and Wednesdays I will do these tasks; on Tuesdays and Thursdays I will tackle this; on Fridays and Saturdays I will work on this; and on Sundays I will rest, relax, refresh, and recuperate. Another option is to break up your workday into chunks or blocks of time (i.e., from 7-10 am I will do this, from 10 am-12 noon I will perform these tasks, and so forth). However, if possible, consider starting tasks at a time when you know you'll be least distracted. For example, many people get up early (get there early) or stay up late (stay late) to circumvent disruptions and create a distraction-free environment. Tip: Keep a separate notebook for each project/activity to ensure copious note keeping (e.g., task lists, system passwords, itemized financials, etc.). There is nothing more distracting than losing information or forgetting details and passwords.

- Another point to consider is your personality type when it comes to your personal projects. If you know that you are not a morning person and work better in the afternoon, then plan tasks during that time— or you can just *get over yourself* and *make it happen*. The *desire* to be comfortable in the quest to achieve your goals and fulfill your duties will hold you back. As a result, you'll inevitably become your greatest distraction. When you are truly *committed*, your main concern is not to placate your personality or coddle your comfortability. Whether you are an introvert or extrovert, personality type A, B, C or D, you make it happen because your drive, your passion, your aim, and your purpose are greater than you.

- Align your long-term goals with your short-term goals to stay on track. For example, a 3-year long-term goal should be aligned with what you do on a daily, weekly, or monthly basis. For instance, if you want to be debt free in three years, then budget, reduce your spending, earn as much as you can and pay down debt regularly and consistently. What you do now in the short-term will take you where you want to go in the long-term.

- Know what you are going to focus on daily—write it down, work hard, and win. If you have no object in sight—no *objecti*ve or vision in life, you have nothing to focus on. And when you have no goal to achieve, you may feel like your life has no meaning.

- Be productive with your mind and time. Maximize time expended by merging tasks when possible to boost input and output such as doing laundry while listening to an informative audio book. I love 'laundry and learn' days.

- Lastly, stick to the endeavors you committed to and stay focused. For instance, if you start a new project or venture, don't give up so easily when you are distracted and discouraged by the rejections, denials, lack of support/responses, mishaps, and mistakes. These internal and external distractions oftentimes make you want to quit and give up too soon. Don't flip flop and engage in herky-jerky habits by starting and then stopping. If you commit to something, give it everything you've got for a committed time and if it doesn't work out, regroup and evaluate what you can change or if you should continue to press forward with the time and resources you have. Oftentimes, tangible success is slow.

There are three things that are compulsory and efficacious to defeating distractions: (1) Discipline (determination), (2) diligence, and (3) discernment. These will enable you to **bang those dang distractions** *and hit your targets successfully.*

"Do the thing and you will have the power."
– Ralph Waldo Emerson

True productivity inherently involves meaning, purpose, and value. For example, you can be more productive by sitting still in silence and meditating to refresh your mind than you can by aimlessly scrolling on social media. *Productivity is* the mother of progress, profitability, and prosperity. When you have a goal, you have a purpose and will be happier and more fulfilled in life as you aim for goals and achieve successful outcomes. However, to minimize disappointments, know that just because you aim does not always mean that you'll hit your targets and achieve—but the important thing is that you tried. Not achieving (hitting your targets) does not negate productivity, but not trying does. Trying produces movement to get you closer to accomplishing your goals. However, don't just try, try hard without the distractions. Aim high!

"I can accept failure. Everyone fails at something. But I can't accept not trying (no hard work)."
– Michael Jordan

The *habit of productivity* is the best habit one can possess because it is profitable beyond measure—not just in the area of money, but profitable for your character, integrity, reputation, self-esteem, freedom, autonomy, family, legacy, largesse, and so much more... yielding immeasurable and meaningful results while combating those *Dang Distractions.*

Good physical, emotional, mental, and spiritual health are derived from good habits.

Discipline distractions so that you won't become broken, bitter or too busy; do not allow them to usurp your authority. Oppose and overcome undistracted and undeterred.

On the next page you'll find a summary of the Top 15 distractions and the weapons (defense) for defeating them. The majority of these weapons can already be found deep within you and are activated when you initiate the *power of perspective* and the *focus of faith*. Note that the knowledge defense is only effective when you *attain* AND *apply* it. Wisdom is knowing how and when to apply what you know while *learning* and *leaning* on the divine source of all truth *who* brings understanding and revelation.

Use these defenses to **persevere** in life (**per**sist even when **severe**). You have the power to control your destiny without allowing distractions to bring 'dis'-harmony into your world. Build balance daily—one step at a time... stay on course, stay on track and always walk in agreement with your duties, goals, and dreams. Focus to finish strong!

Life is too short to live distracted.

*"We must accept finite **disappointment**, but never lose infinite **hope**." - Martin Luther King, Jr.*

Top 15 Distractions

*"Man must evolve for all human **conflict** a method which rejects revenge, aggression, and retaliation. The foundation of such a method is **love**."* - Martin Luther King, Jr.

DISTRACTION	DEFENSE (Oppose/Overcome)
1.Daily tasks and trifles	Wisdom, Discipline (self-control)
2.Debt/Dollars	Knowledge, Wisdom, Discipline (self-control)
3.Deficiency	Knowledge, Faith, Courage
4.Deliberations/Debates/ Disputes/Discussions	Wisdom, Knowledge, Love
5.Disease	Knowledge, Faith, Discipline (self-control)
6.Disorders/Disabilities	Knowledge, Faith, Courage
7.Disparity	Justice, Courage, Love, Wisdom
8.Doubt/Dread/Distress/ Desperation	Faith, Hope, Courage
9.Dysfunction	Knowledge, Faith, Hope, Courage
10.Death/Devastation	Faith, Hope, Courage
11.Drama	Discipline (self-control)
12.Devices	Wisdom, Discipline (self-control)
13.Disappointments	Wisdom, Faith, Hope
14.Desires	Wisdom, Discipline (self-control)
15.Decisions	Wisdom, Knowledge, Discipline (self-control)

What is distracting you (internally/externally)?

_____

_____

_____

_____

_____

How do you PLAN to overcome these distractions
utilizing the defenses mentioned (be specific)?

_____

_____

_____

_____

_____

List some practical steps that you can do to detach
yourself from unnecessary distractions?

_____

_____

_____

_____

_____

Imagine yourself having lived a fully disciplined and
undistracted life. What goals would you have attained and
what dreams would you be living now?

_____

_____

_____

_____

_____

_____

Duty and Distraction Assessment

Activity: _____

This assessment aims to identify duty and distraction activities. Note: Be specific and honest about your motive for engaging in the activity. Write "Yes" (Y) or "No" (N) to answer the questions below.

1. Does this activity serve my family (i.e., contributes to quality time, creates something meaningful and lasting, provides for their well-being, etc.)? _____

2. Does this activity improve me physically, emotionally, mentally, or intellectually? _____

3. Does this activity contribute to my overall purpose such as my passion or definite major purpose* or does it contribute to my purpose as a wife/husband, mother, father, employee, business owner, etc.) _____

4. Does this activity bring me closer to my faith and associated principles and values? _____

5. Does this activity move me closer to my goals, ideas, and dreams? _____

6. Does this activity or will this activity make me a better person (consider morals, values, principles)? _____

7. Does this activity or will this activity benefit others in a meaningful way? ____

If you have more "Yes" answers than "No" answers, this activity is more likely to be a duty. If you have more "No" answers than "Yes" answers, this activity could be a distraction.

*Term derived from Napoleon Hill

"That's the whole story. Here now is my final conclusion: Fear God and obey his commands, for this is everyone's **duty***."* Ecclesiastes 12:13 NLT

"The husband must fulfill his **duty** *to his wife, and likewise also the wife to her husband."*
1 Corinthians 7:3 NASB

"So be careful how you live. Don't live like fools, but like those who are wise. **Make the most of every opportunity** *in these evil days."*
Ephesians 5:15-16 NLT

"But be sure that everything is done properly and in order." 1 Corinthians 14:40 NLT

"Pay careful attention to your own work, for then you will get the satisfaction of a job well done*, and you won't need to compare yourself to anyone else. For we are each responsible for our own conduct."* Galatians 6:5 NLT

Notes

Chapter 1

1. Proverbs 30:15 NLT

2. Proverbs 27:3 NLT

Chapter 2

1. Ecclesiastes 9:10 NLT

Chapter 3

1. Proverbs 23:7 KJV

2. Proverbs 26:22 NLT

3. Rushworth M. Kidder. How Good People Make Tough Choices. Revised Edition. Resolving the Dilemmas of Ethical Living - November 24, 2009

Chapter 4

1. Michael E. Gerber. The E-Myth Revisited: Why Most Small Business Don't Work and What to Do About It - October 12, 2004